Blackpool and Fleetw

by Raymond Sankey and K.J. Norm

GW00731840

Dalesman Books
1989

The Dalesman Publishing Company Ltd.
Clapham, Lancaster LA2 8EB
First Published 1989

ISBN: 0 85206 988 X

Printed by Smiths of Bradford

Contents

Front cover: With the tide out, fully clothed youngsters are able to indulge in the traditional seaside pastime of building sand castles. Even boots are being worn! The scene is dominated by the Tower and the Big Wheel in between which is the Palatine Hotel. (2486)

Back cover: Central tramway tracks with the pedestrian area on one side and the roadway on the other can be clearly seen. Horses are plentiful and street cleaners are busy on the right cleaning up after them. On the right hand side of the road is part of the famous Golden Mile which began in 1897 when palmists, phrenologists, quack doctors, mock auctions and similar ventures were banned from the sands. The result of this was that these traders moved to the other side of the road where they bought houses and set up business in the front garden. (4288)

A means of loading pleasure boats was by horse-drawn boat-cars, transfer from which can only have been slightly less hazardous than the portable gangways. (5237)

Introduction

In the early part of the 19th century Sir Peter Hesketh Fleetwood masterminded a plan to build a port and holiday resort on land he owned on the estuary of the River Wyre, the town to carry his name and be known as Fleetwood.

In 1835 a railway company, The Preston and Wyre Railway Company, was formed to link the new town with the national railway network at Preston and a single line running through the towns of Kirkham and Poulton was opened on July 15th, 1840.

Whilst Fleetwood did develop into a port of some importance and became a busy centre of the fishing industry, its popularity as a holiday resort never realised the grandiose expectations of its founder. Instead, it was the neighbouring genteel Victorian watering place of Blackpool, a few miles along the coast to the South, which was destined to overtake Fleetwood in popularity to become one of the major holiday resorts in the country, if not in the world.

The arrival of the railway in Blackpool in 1846, by means of a branch line leaving the Preston and Wyre Railway at Poulton and running into a station in Talbot Road paved the way for holiday makers and excursionists from the industrial towns of Lancashire and Yorkshire to arrive in Blackpool in their thousands.

Enterprising businessmen and land owners of the region rose to the challenge to create from the original quiet resort a bustling, thriving, holiday metropolis with hotels, boarding houses, shops and holiday attractions to house, feed and amuse this great floating population.

For a time, before the coming of the railway, steamers plying between Barrow and Liverpool called at Blackpool and it seems appropriate that, by sea, should come Edward Sankey, father of one of the authors, a master printer and photographer from Barrow who travelled regularly on the Furness Railway Company's paddle steamers sailing between Barrow and Fleetwood photographing passengers on the morning crossings and selling prints to them when they returned in the evening.

That period before the Great War of 1914–1918 was the Golden Age of the picture post card and Mr. Sankey, aware of the multitudes of visitors to Blackpool, sought to capitalise on this readymade market by taking photographs of the town, its shopping areas, its hotels, its streets of boarding houses and its amusements, for the purpose of making post cards for sale in Blackpool, to the holidaymakers.

Most of these post cards have, by now, probably been destroyed but fortunately the original negatives still exist and it is from these that the illustrations in this book have been made.

In making our selection of pictures we have tried as far as possible to avoid those already seen in similar publications and we believe that most of the illustrations are being seen for the first time since they appeared as picture post cards in those far off days at the beginning of the century.

If perusal of these pages gives as much pleasure to the reader as preparation did to the authors then our efforts have been well worthwhile.

R. Sankey
K.J. Norman
September 1989

(Negative numbers have been included with the photographs).

Fleetwood

Passengers are leaving the Wyre Ferry at Knott End after crossing from Fleetwood, on the other side of the estuary. In the background can be seen the North Euston Hotel, the Lower light and the life-boat house. (5158)

The tiny wooden steam ferry boat *Progress* is tied up against the landing at Fleetwood, and passengers are embarking for the return trip to Knott End. There were two boats operating the service, the other one being named *Wyresdale*. (4764)

A first glimpse of Fleetwood as it would have appeared to visitors arriving by sea on steamers from the Isle of Man or Barrow. The London and North Western Railway Company's imposing North Euston Hotel dominates a scene almost certainly taken from one of the Furness Railway Company's cross-bay paddle steamers. (2818)

The pilots Watch House on the Fleetwood landing stage and a group of harbour staff.
Note the megaphone to transmit verbal instructions from shore to ship during berthing
operations. (1073)

The Lancashire and Yorkshire and London and North-Western joint railway station at Fleetwood was situated adjacent to the steamer landing stages at the North end of the promenade. Through here poured thousands of tourists from Blackpool to join the paddle steamers of the Furness Railway Company in connection with the Company's "Outer Circular Tour" which commenced with a trip across the bay to Barrow before embarking on a journey to Ambleside and Coniston by train, lake steamer and horse bus.

The round trip starting from Blackpool Talbot Road station at 10.00am, did not get back until 8.45pm. The fare was 12/6d (62½p) first class and 7/9d (37½p) third class and it must have been an exhausting experience. (2174)

The spacious booking hall at Fleetwood with its refreshment rooms, steamer booking office and staff posing in front of the camera. (2173)

Crowds watch a display in the Marine Gardens which seems to involve a lady with a decorated bicycle. Notices on the perimeter fence around the tennis courts extol the virtues of Devona Flake pipe tobacco at 4½d; invite holidaymakers to visit the Bourne Arms Hotel at Knott End with its "Large Grill Room" and "Bowling Green"; or sample the Mount Hotel on the Central Promenade "The Best Hotel in the District". The starting point for "Electric Cars to and from Blackpool every few minutes" is indicated by a pointing finger. The railway station and docks are in the background and the occasion, according to the negative envelope is "The Fleetwood Regatta". (2237)

The Mount Hotel seen from the Mount with the promenade on the right curving away towards Blackpool. (5246)

There are few people about to disturb the peace in this 1920's view from the Mount. (9752)

Another picture from the same era showing the pavilion on the Mount. (9750)

The Fylde coast's other tower, Fleetwood's famous landmark the Pharos lighthouse, a lighthouse in the middle of a street. The railway station and promenade are in the background. (2181)

A busy promenade is seen from the No[rth]
Euston Hotel, the dress of the ladies and t[he]
style of the perambulators point to this be[ing]
a scene at the beginning of the century. T[he]
Lower light in the centre was used in
conjunction with the Pharos light (see 21[8])
as an aid to navigation for vessels enterin[g]
the port. The booth on the left of the li[ght]
with the semi-circular roof sold Angell [&]
Ventella's Pure Ice Cream and the who[le]
scene suggests a warm sunny day. (217[ ])

Fleetwood had its own pier, albeit muc[h]
shorter than those at Blackpool. (2654)

The banner above the entrance to the pier informs potential customers that the Anglo Indians will perform at 2.45 and 7.30pm. On the right a trawler can just be seen heading for the fishing grounds. (2686)

Crowds throng the promenade, the d‹
and railway station are on the left, th
lifeboat house is on the right, with P‹
in the centre background in this pict
taken from the pier. (2233)

Trawler FD 372 *Eddystone* leaving
Fleetwood for the fishing grounds while
Knott End ferry comes in to Fleetwood.
(8429)

A fine action shot of fish being unloaded from a trawler of Fleetwood's deep sea fishing fleet, which in its heyday numbered nearly 150 vessels. The sight of the fleet putting to sea drew holidaymakers to watch. On their return, each ship would signal its safe home-coming with blasts on its siren. (2231)

Trawler FD 357 *Princess Juliana* leaving Fleetwood. Knott End in background. (8420)

Harry Matto's concert party The Rigmaroles perform in the Marine Gardens to an audience seated traditionally in deck chairs. There are six performers on stage and one wonders if the netting enclosure is to keep intruders out or the audience in. A closer look, however, reveals that the seating is arranged on one of the tennis courts. A 1920's photograph. (D706)

The tennis courts in the Marine Gardens, which lay between the Mount and the Promenade, the dress of the players and strollers indicating that this is another taken in the 1920's. (9748)

A practically deserted Albert Square where tobacconist Sharman on the left was an agent for Masta pipes. (4261)

Princess Street and Foxhall Square with Dale Street on the left and the old gas works in the background. Two men are able to converse in the middle of the road with little danger from the horse and cart or the lone cyclist. The poster on the left in front of A.V. Barker's provision shop advertises Alick Chumley and A. Russell-Davies appearing in "The Little Damozel" at Her Majesty's Opera House Winter Gardens Blackpool commencing Monday 27th May 1913. (4669)

Blackpool North

Cliffs have always had an attraction for people on holiday and those at Bispham were no exception. Palmists, fortunetellers, phrenologists and quack doctors were favourite forms of entertainment with the holidaymakers of yesteryear and two of the booths in this picture testify to this popularity. On the left "Madame Catherine Townsend, The Italian Gypsy, Late of South Shore and Birmingham", a self-styled character reading expert, gave advice on health and business, whilst almost next door Madame Flora invited consultation and would "give advice on how to obtain health, wealth and happiness". Also in the scene is a booth offering "Your Photograph for One Penny". A crossbench tram on its way to Fleetwood has paused at Bispham station. (5238)

Between Fleetwood and Blackpool are three small resorts the most northerly of which is Cleveleys. This picture shows the shops in Victoria Road, butcher, chemist, draper, newsagent, barber and on the other side of the road, grocer. Could the lady on the left pushing the bath chair be taking her invalid father for a haircut? (4503)

On the cliffs at Cleveleys stood the substantial Cleveleys Hydro Hotel where the more affluent holidaymakers could enjoy the peace and quiet of the village and yet be only a few miles from the entertainments on offer at the nearby resorts. (4519)

The distinctive but not necessarily
attractive Norbreck Hall Hydro, another
haven of peace on the cliffs North of
Blackpool for the well-to-do, was, as its
name implies at the village of Norbreck
about one mile South of Cleveleys on the
Blackpool-Fleetwood Tramroad. The
nameboard of the tram station can just be
seen on the extreme left of the picture. (5229)

Guests enjoy a game of tennis on the private
courts of the Hydro which in the 1930's also
had its own private indoor swimming pool.
On the left the grass is being cut by a single
horse-power mower and in the foreground
are the double tracks of the tramway in their
special reservation.

Opened in July 1898 the route started at
Gynn Square in Blackpool and at that time
passengers were transferred from the
Blackpool trams, which terminated in Talbot
Square, by horse bus. Later in 1898 the
tramroad was extended into the centre of
Blackpool by way of Dickson Road to Talbot
Road station. (5231)

The stylish building on the right bearing the name "Uncle Tom's Cabin" is a reminder of one of the earliest places of entertainment in Blackpool. Standing on the cliffs close to the sea the original "Uncle Tom's Cabin" had in its heyday a dancing pavilion with its own orchestra, a bar selling wines and ales, a refreshment room at which could be purchased "Biscuits, Sweet Cakes, Sweets, Nuts, Lemonade and Ginger Beer, which for quality and price are second-to-none ever offered to the public".

A telescope was also available through which views of the Lake District, Wales and the surrounding area could be obtained, whilst mounted on the roof were three wooden figures representing the characters Uncle Tom, Little Eva and Topsy from the book "Uncle Tom's Cabin". Erosion of the cliffs caused part of the structure to collapse and the remainder was demolished in 1907. (5292)

The elegant terrace of houses in Queens Gate with a Standard De-Luxe tram of Blackpool Corporation Tramways at the Gynn Inn terminus in the distance. The car outside the Belvedere is a model T Ford, registration number N 8266, its driver wearing goggles and the passengers well wrapped up against the cold in contrast to the flannel clad young men, one of whom is carrying a tennis racquet. (4344)

Building the sunken gardens North of Gynn Square during the construction of the Queens Promenade towards Bispham, where the cliffs were being re-inforced at the same time. In the distance can be seen Gynn Inn and Queens Gate. (5295)

The end of the Corporation tram track, which reached Gynn Inn in 1900, with its ornate tram shelter which also served as a refreshment kiosk and public toilet. Double deck "Dreadnought" tram No. 23 is waiting to begin its journey along the promenade to South Shore. Although the Corporation track ended within a few feet of those of the Blackpool and Fleetwood Company there was no inter-connection and passengers had to cross the Square on foot to join the Fleetwood tram. This state of affairs continued until the Corporation acquired the Fleetwood line in 1919 when a curve was constructed to link the two systems. A year or two after the amalgamation the Gynn Inn was pulled down to allow for re-alignment of the junction to permit the running of double decker trams to Fleetwood. Note the cows grazing in the field in the background to the right of the tram. (4541)

Another view at the Gynn Inn showing the Duke of Cambridge Hotel and its bowling green at the end of Dickson Road. (4638)

A Corporation Standard De-Luxe car has just arrived at the end of the line at Queens Gate and passengers are crossing the Square to join the Fleetwood tram. The close proximity of the two lines is apparent from this picture. On the right a "Dreadnought" tram is starting its journey to South Shore along the promenade. (4639)

Occupying a prominent position on the North promenade is the Imperial Hydropathic Hotel, still there and sometimes used by the Conservative Party when they are holding their Annual Conference in Blackpool. (4642)

A scene in Regent Square, known nowadays as Cocker Square, looking along Cocker Street. A sign on the building on the corner of General Street, entering on the right, proclaims "Baths" in large letters – a word which is repeated on the chimney beyond. The chemists shop on the right belonged to Oliver L. Jackson M.P.S. who sold Vanishing Cream in jars at 7½d and 1/6d, also a New Beauty Secret at 1/6d and 2/9d per jar. Cocker Street perpetuates the name of the Cocker family, pioneers of the development of the Central area which culminated in the opening of Victoria Terrace in 1837, a block containing shops, a library, a news room and a billiard room. A son of the family, Dr. W.H. Cocker became the first mayor of Blackpool. (4439)

Princess Parade with Albert Terrace on the right carried vehicular traffic past the Metropole Hotel to the promenade beyond, a function it still performs today. Of interest is the Princess Theatre in Albert Terrace. (4488)

The sea washes against the new promenade extension from North Pier, round the Hotel Metropole, to Cocker Street. Begun in September 1910 the space between the new and old sea walls was filled with sand being deposited in large quantities on the beaches at the Southern end of the town as a result of various sea defences built in that area. James Brodie, Borough Engineer at the time, decided that transport of the filling some two miles along the promenade by road would be very costly so he built a standard gauge railway line, laying the sleepers and track on the ashphalt surface between the tramlines and the pedestrian way without any ballast. This railway, which soon became known locally as "The Sands Express" began work in January 1911, completion of the filling being planned by Easter and the arrival of the first visitors. At the height of the operation five 0-6-0 saddle tank locomotives and 62 side-tipping wagons were in use. (4274)

Holidaymakers throng the new promenade, which was opened by H.R.H. Princess Louise on May 2nd 1912. The Hotel Metropole was originally known as Baileys Hotel and was opened in 1776. The current hotel has been considerably enlarged and bears little resemblance to the earlier building. (5289)

The new promenade provided walkway[s?] four separate levels and visitors are ma[king] use of all tiers to sit or stroll in the sunsh[ine] (4327)

In the opposite direction lies Talbot Sq[uare] and the Tower. The flag on the extreme [right?] flies over the entrance to the North Pier. [The?] dress seems quite unsuitable for a su[nny] day. (4342)

The Palace and Tower, including holidaymakers on the North Pier. The Tower, a 520 foot high replica of the Eiffel Tower in Paris, was one of several projected for Northern sea-side towns but in the event it was the only one ever completed. Built on the site of an aquarium, menagerie and aviary owned by Dr. W.H. Cocker, the foundation stone was laid by the local Member of Parliament on 25th September 1891 and the opening was at Whitsuntide 1894. The aquarium, menagerie and aviary had been kept open during construction to provide revenue but after completion they were incorporated into the new structure alongside the ballroom and famous Tower Circus. (5235)

The famous Blackpool skyline seen from the North Pier showing from left to right the dome of the Winter Gardens, the Giant Ferris Wheel at the Winter Gardens, the Palace Buildings and the Tower. (5236)

The Tower roof gardens provide a haven of rest where visitors could sit and admire the tropical vegetation even when the weather outside was inclement. (4676)

A look inside the menagerie where, according to the late Stanley Holloway in his well-known monologue, little Albert Ramsbottom was eaten by a lion. (4672)

Obviously a Royal occasion in Talbot Square, the Clifton Hotel and Square decorated, crowds lining the Square and children in the foregound waving Union Jacks, the police are also in evidence to keep order. The domed structure on the left is a drinking fountain. Thomas Clifton of the Talbot-Clifton family was responsible for the development of this area laying out Talbot Road to run from his estate in Layton right through to the promenade, terminating in a new square which he bequeathed to the town. An inn standing on one corner of the Square was renamed Clifton Arms in his honour, later to be rebuilt into the Clifton Hotel, seen here, and the Square became Talbot Square thus perpetuating the family name. (4286)

Blackpool Central Area

The Railway Hotel stood on the corner of Talbot Road and Maybelle Avenue, the tramlines curving in the foreground are leaving Abingdon Street. Note the ornate lamp standards doubling as poles to carry the overhead powerlines for the trams. (4470)

Talbot Road station, built in 1898 to replace an original station of 1846, had an imposing frontage with no less than three clocks. Until the arrival of the railway in 1846 travellers to Blackpool left the Fleetwood train at Poulton and finished their journey to Blackpool by horse-bus. It was Thomas Clifton, already mentioned, who was responsible for the laying of a single track line from Poulton on the Fleetwood route, to Blackpool, which was opened on April 29th 1846 and doubled in 1868. The station pictured here was replaced, in 1974, by a smaller station built on the site of the old excursion platforms. (4876)

An interior view of the station at Talbot Road with its lofty twin arched roof covering seven platforms. In addition there were eight more excursion platforms with a separate entrance. (2191)

The station entrance in Dickson Road protected from the weather by this massive canopy beneath which is an early taxi registration number FR 492. A notice on wall of the Station Hotel on the left advertises horse racing at Clifton Park, South Shore and in the distance a tram waiting at the Blackpool and Fleetwood Tramroad terminus. (4400)

The Central Public Library stands at the junction of Abingdon Street and Queen Street and looks very new in this picture. Horse drawn landaus wait for fares and a board on the right advertises free admission to a "Special Exhibition of Paintings". (4472)

At the "Y" junction where Talbot Road and Clifton Street – seen here – leave Talbot Square stood one of the towns earliest theatres, the Theatre Royal, opened in 1868. Yates's Wine Lodge now occupies the site but the canopies of the old theatre are still in position. To the rear is the Post Office in Abingdon Street and the destination board on the tram is "Hospital". (4457)

Bank Hey Street from the rear of the Tower building looking towards Victoria Street, below the ornate shop frontage on the right are three brass balls of the pawnbroker, a sign not often seen nowadays, but an establishment which could have been a lifesaver in those days, if the holiday cost more than was budgeted for. (4493)

The Post Office in Abingdon Street opposite the junction with Clifton Street was built on the site of the Union Baptist Chapel. Next door are the premises of Taylors Drug Company Ltd. Chemists to the People, offering "Rose and Lily Cream for Sunburn, 3½d. and 7½d. per bottle." Taylors later amalgamated with another chain of chemists to become Timothy White's and Taylors before this was absorbed into the Boots empire. (4407)

A picture of Abingdon Street from its junction with Church Street which is full of interest. A toast rack tram on a circular tour waits on the double track for approaching De-Luxe car No. 65 to pass before taking the single line to Clifton Street. On the left is what appears to be a hay cart, why would this be in such a busy thoroughfare? The advertisements too are fascinating, at the Palace, commencing on Monday August 25th, "The One, The Only, Vesta Tilley", whilst at the Tower on Sunday August 31st, Miss Agnes Nicholls soprano with the Blackpool Ladies Orpheus Choir and the Tower Grand Orchestra directed by Mr. J. Woof Gaggs is giving a "Grand Special Concert". On the corner beneath the hoardings a gift shop offers "Celebrated Strong Watches" at 2/9d. (approx. 14p) each. (4639A)

The promenade is seen from the top deck of a tram as it approaches the Tower.
Blackpool's first promenade ran from the site of the Tower northwards to Church Street
a distance of about 200 yards and was 3 yards wide. The North Pier, oldest of the three
piers, was known as the Blackpool Pier when it was opened on May 23rd 1863. On the
right the Royal Hotel and Market were later to become the Woolworth building. (5518)

An Edwardian fashion parade on the promenade in front of the Lane Ends Hotel – see 4473 – gentlemen in dark suits wearing a variety of headgear, bowler hats, trilby's, straw boaters and caps, the ladies in long coats and dresses are also all wearing hats. Starring at the Palace, Wilkie Bard. (4487)

The promenade seen from a first floor window in the Palace. Central Pier is in the distance. (4494)

Taken from the upper storey of an unidentified hotel which was the Official Quarters of the National Cyclists Union a view of Church Street looking towards Bank Hey Street with the dome of the Grand Theatre just visible on the left. A delivery of beer is being made from a motor dray in the centre. On the right is the drapers and outfitters belonging to Donnelly and Sons. Note the sunblinds on all of the shops on the right hand side of the street. (4499)

This part of Central Beach has changed considerably since this picture of the Palatine Hotel was taken. An amusemen arcade now stands at the junction of Centi Beach and Hounds Hill. The building in th background beneath the wheel was one the early theatres, the Borough Theatre a Concert Hall, which at the time of this photograph was Bannisters Arcade. Late: returned to its original role as a theatre Feldmans, and is now the C&A store. N the boot black sitting on the pavement the right. (4484)

The Victoria Hotel at the corner of Central Beach and Brunswick Street sold R. Seed and Cos. Radcliffe Ales and Stout. The hotels own livery stables at the rear are a reminder that most traffic in the town was horse-drawn in those far off days before the Great War. (4326)

Adelaide Street was a favourite viewpoint for photographers of the day giving, as it did from its junction with Alfred Street, this shot of the Wheel and Tower superimposed. (4303)

Central Drive was the route of the Blackpc — Lytham and St. Anne's trams in and out of the town centre. This view looking toward Hounds Hill, with Hornby Road on the righ has Central Station left. The young and not so young pose for the camera. (4451)

Further along Central Drive E. Thomas sol Colmans mustard and Darbyshire's brea whilst above his shop was a billiard hall with five tables. (4459)

A wonderful fashion picture of ladies in Church Street crossing the end of Coronation Street with a child in a bassinette, very different from the modern folding baby stroller. On the left is the impressive frontage of the Winter Gardens facing Victoria Street and on the right Bentleys Ltd. sold ladies wear. The building beyond the tobacconist's shop was the old Post Office. (4444)

The Winter Gardens complex is built on the site of "Bank Hey" the residence of Dr. W.H. Cocker at the top of Victoria Street. At the opening ceremony the mayors of 68 different towns took part in a grand procession arranged by Dr. Cocker and guest of honour was the Lord Mayor of London for whom Dr. Cocker laid on a special train to transport the state coaches and nine horses to Blackpool. Sarah Bernhardt was once booked to appear at the Winter Gardens in the play "Lady of the Camellias" but the accoustics in the pavilion were so poor that the actress was unable to make herself heard and she walked out at the end of the first act and refused to return. (4296)

Albert Road was photographed on 17th August 1922. The gable end next to the Albert Restaurant has a tablet which reads "Clarance Livery Stables 1892" but keeping pace with the changing times the building has been converted to the motor age and a new sign tells that it has become "Walker Taylor and Sons Clarence Garage (note the different spelling of Clarence) from which Pride of the Road Motors left daily for all parts. (6898)

The giant Ferris Wheel was built by the Winter Gardens Company as a counter attraction to the Tower. Standing 220 feet high it was opened in August 1896 and had 30 carriages each seating 30 people. The ride, which lasted 15 minutes, was one circuit of the wheel, punctuated by 30 stops to unload and reload each car as it reached the bottom. The fare was 6d. (2½p) but the wheel never was a serious rival to the Tower as a money spinner and in 1901 there was talk of dismantling it. The cost of this was so prohibitive that the wheel was operated at a loss for many years before being dismantled in late 1928. (4441)

Visitors and a page boy watch the photographer under the vaulted roof of the Winter Gardens. In the background is the entrance to the circle of the Opera House and on the right are a row of souvenir stalls. Also on the right a booth offers the "Largest Photo in the World" at 6d. each and post cards at 6 for 1/– (5p), all ready in 10 minutes, using "Mercury Vapour Photography" which, presumably, refers to the type of lamps used for illumination of the sitter. A notice in the foreground advertises the Blackpool Musical Festival in October 1913 thereby dating the picture. (4436)

The interior of the Empress Ballroom, opened in 1897 showing the inadequacies of the photographic materials of the day, the absence of an anti-halation backing on the plates allowing the windows to burn out. The picture does however capture the ornate elegance of the interior with its arched roof and inlaid wooden floor. Over the stage a patriotic sign proclaims "For The Dear Homeland". (4482)

Of all the amusements and entertainments on offer, the beach was, without doubt, the most popular with the holiday crowds as this scene on Central beach shows. The bathing machines of H. and E. Smith, protecting the modesty of the lady bathers, line the water's edge, ice cream vendors, donkey rides and oyster stalls, all vie for custom on the sands and the promenade is thronged with people. (4276)

The photographer has obviously rolled up his trousers, taken off his shoes and socks and gone into the water to get this shot of children playing in the shallows. The incoming tide is compressing the crowd on to an ever decreasing strip of sand, but ice cream vendor Dominic Perry "established over 50 years" is clinging to his pitch. The dress of the people on the sands contrasts strongly with the liberated beach wear of the 1980's. (4434)

Another very popular attraction was the boat trip on the bay and here one of the sailing boats is being loaded by means of a portable gangway. Bathing machines and the North Pier are in the background. (4418)

Despite being held by boatmen standing up to their waists in the sea, boarding a boat in the voluminous dresses of the times must have been an adventure in itself. (4284)

The entrance to Central Pier where the Premier Pierrots under the direction of Fred Allandale were performing at 2.45 and 7.30pm. Originally known as the South Jetty the pier was opened in May 1868 but being at that time some way from the town centre it was not well patronised. In order to try to boost revenue a steamer *Lady of the Lake*, an unusual name for a sea-going vessel, was introduced to sail to Southport, but it was not until the introduction of dancing on the pier that it really became popular. Note the gentleman having his shoes cleaned just behind the carriage. (5102)

The sands on Central beach are becoming uncomfortably congested as the advancing tide drives the holidaymakers back towards the promenade. Bathing machines and pleasure craft are all in evidence with Central Pier in the distance. (4461)

The new sea wall, built when the promenade was widened in the early 1900's, can be seen clearly in this view Southwards from Central Pier towards Lytham Road and the Manchester Hotel, the rising tide has covered the sand and driven the crowds on to the promenade, on which a "Dreadnought" tram is on its way south. A few people are sitting on the steps waiting for the tide to recede and a few venturesome souls are paddling in the shallow water. (4283)

Blackpool South Shore

South Shore station behind the camera and the tram is bound for Lytham, the route to Blackpool is off to the right. (4392)

This attractive building is Linden Lea and it stands on the promenade at the corner of Dean Street near Victoria Pier. (4670)

Woodfield Road South Shore running between Lytham Road and the Promenade, with children on tricycles hurrying to be in the picture. Street scenes such as this and others in the collection were popular with visitors as the street in which they were staying was a favourite subject to send to the less fortunate friends and family who had to remain at home. In a town of around 35,000 inhabitants, at that time, which had to sleep 250,000 visitors during the season, most houses offered some kind of accommodation so most of the streets came in front of the lenses of the post card photographers. (4381)

The corner shop at the junction of Crystal Road and Bolton Street shows on its hoardings and notices an intersting glimpse of every day life in those times. A billboard for the Daily News proclaims "Suffragette Pilgrimage, Triumphant Conclusion", Answers announce "Valuable Prizes Given Away in This Town Today" and Home Chat, not to be outdone, is giving away "Air Balloons Free". Sea trips to Douglas from North and Central Piers are advertised. Mr. Ashcroft in his dual purpose shop stocks Colmans starch, HP sauce and "Columbia River Salmon Just Arrived". (4290)

Victoria Pier was opened in 1893 and is now known as South Pier. When this picture was taken Ackeroyds Band was playing in the pavilion and sand castle making was in full swing on the beach. (4398)

South Promenade and the beach are seen from Victoria Pier, the crowds are not so dense as those previously seen on pictures of the Central beaches. (4357)

An early picture of the Pleasure Beach when it actually was on the beach. Starting as a fairground on the South Shore, the Pleasure Beach was developed by John Outhwaite and Walter George Bean when the extension of the tramway to South Shore meant that end of the town was in easy reach of holidaymakers previously confined to the central area. The Sir Hiram Maxim Flying Machine seen here opened in 1904 and was one of the first mechanical rides, the others being a scenic railway and "River Caves of the World". (2195)

Almost certainly the same occasion as (9046) page 60, but seen this time from a vantage point on the South Pier with the new outdoor pool in prominence. A greatly extended Pleasure Beach can be seen with the Water Chute, Virginia Reel, Helter Skelter and Rainbow Wheel visible in addition to the original Flying Machine and Scenic Railway. After the extension of the tramway to the Pleasure Beach the destination boards were changed on the trams from South Shore to Pleasure Beach. (9045)

The outdoor swimming pool and the extension of the promenade to the Pleasure Beach were opened in June 1923 and this picture, taken from the Casino, with crowds of spectators lining the promenade would appear to record this event. Note the large number of motor vehicles and only two horse-drawn landaus. (9046)

Trams have been much in evidence throughout this book and Blackpool is the only British town still to operate this form of public transport.

Toast rack No. 84 is on the promenade service but the main usage of this type was on the Circular Tours, advertisements for which can be seen on several pictures. Starting in Talbot Square, this was routed along the promenade to Station Road, into Lytham Road, then Waterloo Road to Whitegate Road where a photographer was waiting to take a group picture. From there the route entered Church Street, turned into Abingdon Street and Clifton Street before returning to Talbot Square. (5518)

A "Dreadnought" tram and its crew pose at Gynn Inn before leaving for South Shore. These 45 foot long monsters with double staircases at each end could carry 100 passengers, 86 of them seated. To deal with such a number of people required two conductors but the speed with which they could be loaded and unloaded made them the mainstay of traffic along the promenade from their introduction in 1900 until withdrawal in 1934-5. (4543)

Tram No. 31 has just arrived at the terminus of the Layton route which ran from Talbot Square along Talbot Road to Blackpool's cemetery which can be seen on the right. One of the passengers just alighting is carrying flowers destined no doubt to be laid on the grave of a loved one and the conductor is changing the trolley for the return journey. Called "Marton" boxes, presumably because they were used extensively on the Marton route, they could seat 63 passengers and 15 were built in 1901. (4796)

The first illuminated tram ran on June 22nd 1897 to mark the Diamond Jubilee of Queen Victoria and another was used on the occasion of the opening of the new promenade around the Hotel Metropole by H.R.H. Princess Louise on the 2nd May 1912. This standard class car, as well as being decorated with flags and crowns, had "Long Live Our King and Queen" in lights along the side. Could this have been to mark a Royal visit or a Jubilee? Photographed in a depot, note the early motor bus, carrying the destination board "Layton", at the rear. (9043)

The illuminated tram, out on the promenade at Talbot Square during the illuminations. It is appropriate that it should be posed here as this was the location of Blackpool's first illuminations. Lights were strung between tram poles in Talbot Square and around the Hotel Metropole when the promenade was opened in May 1912. These "lights" were dismantled soon afterwards but were re-erected in September of the same year and lasted until the middle of October to become the first "Blackpool Illuminations". Discontinued during the 1914 – 1918 war years the lights were not re-introduced until 1925 and that is the probable date of this picture. (4679)